The Art of Sugarcraft

MARZIPAN

The Art of Sugarcraft

MARZIPAN

PAT ASHBY

Foreword James Winterflood
Series Editor Joyce Becker
Photography by Melvin Grey and Graham Tann

MEREHURST PRESS
LONDON

Published 1986 by Merehurst Press
5 Great James Street
London WC1N 3DA

ISBN 0 948075 08 2

Designed by Carole Perks
Editorial Assistant Suzanne Ellis
Further assistance provided by Trudie Ballantyne, Rachel Lalley
    and Sara Townshend
Cover photograph by Melvin Grey
Typeset by Filmset
Colour separation by Fotographics Ltd, London-Hong Kong
Printed by New Interlitho S.p.A., Milan

ACKNOWLEDGEMENTS
Pat Ashby would like to thank George, Susan and Justin Ashby and
Barbara Nayler for their help in the preparation of this book.

The publishers would like to thank the following companies for their
help in the preparation of this book:
Cuisena Cookware Limited
Guy, Paul and Company Limited, Unit B4, A1 Industrial Park,
    Little End Road, Eton Scoton, Cambridgeshire, PE19 3JH
Sugarflair Colours Limited
B.R. Mathews, 12 Gipsy Hill, London SE19 1NN
A Piece of Cake, 18 Upper High Street, Thame, Oxon, OX9 2XE
Elizabeth David Limited, 46 Bourne Street, London SW1 and at
    Covent Garden Kitchen Supplies, 3 North Row, The Market,
    London WC2
Orchard Products, 49 Langdale Road, Hove, Sussex, BN3 4HR
John F. Renshaw and Company Limited, Locks Lane, Mitcham, Surrey,
    CR4 2XE
C.E.P. Moulds

Companion volumes:
The Art of Sugarcraft — **CHOCOLATE**
The Art of Sugarcraft — **PIPING**
The Art of Sugarcraft — **SUGAR FLOWERS**

CONTENTS

Being a qualified teacher and cake decorator with a unique creative ability makes Pat Ashby a popular sugarcraft artist, particularly in the areas of marzipan modelling and chocolate work.

London-born Pat began to study cake decorating at Brighton Technical College, where she became proficient in sugarcraft techniques and obtained her teacher's certificate.

A trip to Germany, where every town has its marzipan factory, gave Pat her interest in this area of sugarart. Because marzipan and chocolate are often combined in decorating, she became an expert in chocolate work as well. She now teaches these two subjects, as well as other icing techniques and her students win prizes at all of the sugarcraft exhibitions.

Pat herself prefers to judge competitions rather than enter them. She is a member of the Sugarcraft Guilds of Britain, America, Australia and South Africa, and she is in close contact with sugarcraft artists all over the world. In 1985, she co-authored FINISHING TOUCHES — THE ART OF CAKE DECORATING.

Pat Ashby now lives in Hove with her husband George, a retired engineer. They have three children.

FOREWORD

There are few books on the market which deal exclusively with marzipan and its many uses, although many cake decorating books touch upon the subject in one form or another.

It is always exciting, therefore, when a new book on marzipan is published, especially one which covers such a wide range of techniques and applications.

In this book the author has paid a lot of attention to the requirements of the reader, explaining in detail the techniques and skills that can be developed. There is also inbuilt encouragement to improve expertise, for, no matter how good or clever a person is, there is always room for improvement in some way or another.

As you browse though the pages of this excellent book, your excitement will grow, and your appreciation of the author's craftmanship will become more and more evident.

The many shapes and their varied forms are a delight to see, bringing a breath of fresh air to an old established theme. The colouring is outstanding, giving a bright crisp look to the photographs, which are clear and precise. The backgrounds are uncluttered and enhance the overall appearance.

In some books, modelling is spoiled by poor detail of facial expression which is not always easy to achieve. The author, however, has not only provided us with a wealth of expression, but in the detail she has introduced a feminine touch which makes the figures even more appealing.

I hope you will enjoy this book as much as I have and that you will agree with me when I say that Pat Ashby has created a wonderful marzipan manual.

My greatest admiration to her for this contribution to cake decorating.

JAMES WINTERFLOOD
Development Executive
John F. Renshaw and Co. Ltd.

CATS ON A CUSHION

TYPES OF MARZIPAN

Marzipan is basically a paste made from a mixture of nibbed almonds and sugar. The proportion of almonds to sugar varies according to the manufacturer, and some commercial marzipans include ground apricot or peach kernels or, occasionally, ground soya beans or soyflour. Egg white or whole egg is sometimes added for special purposes. The three most common types of marzipan available are white marzipan, yellow marzipan and raw sugar marzipan.

White marzipan: This is the marzipan used by most cake decorators, and it is usually made from nibbed almonds and sugar only. White marzipan can be used in all sugarcraft calling for marzipan. It takes colour well. As the various brands available in each country may differ slightly, choose a brand which is easy to work with, neither too dry nor too sticky.

Yellow marzipan or almond icing: Yellow marzipan, which is often used to cover rich fruit cakes before icing, has permitted edible colouring added to a basic marzipan recipe. Because of the yellow dye, it does not colour well, and is therefore not recommended for sugarcraft work.

Raw sugar marzipan: Available from health food shops and large supermarkets, this brown marzipan is made from nibbed almonds and unrefined sugar. It is sticky and does not model as well as white marzipan, and it does not take colour well. However, it has a pleasant flavour and can be used to cover cakes or for some marzipan sweets.

BUYING MARZIPAN

Marzipan can be purchased from cake decorating suppliers and from many supermarkets and health food stores. Always buy from a shop which has a rapid turnover, as stale marzipan will be hard and difficult to work with.

Most shops sell marzipan in foil or plastic wrapped packages, in weights of either 250g, 500g. 1kg or ½lb, 1lb, 2lb. Some cake decorating suppliers make up their own packs in varying weights or will sell marzipan by the kilo or pound.

Homemade marzipan

Most cake decorators use commercial marzipan because homemade marzipan is often sticky and more difficult to work with. However, this boiled almond paste has a good flavour and can be used for most sugarcraft work.

Makes about 350g (12oz)
200g (7oz/1¾cups) sugar
120ml (4floz/½cup) water
pinch cream of tartar
150g (5oz/1¼cups) ground almonds
1-2 drops almond essence or extract
1 large egg white
icing (confectioner's) sugar, for dusting

Put the sugar and water in a small saucepan and cook over low heat, stirring occasionally, until the sugar is dissolved.

Add the cream of tartar and quickly bring to the boil. Boil until it reaches a temperature of 116°C (240°F), or soft ball stage.

Remove from the heat and beat until the mixture turns cloudy. Add the ground almonds and the almond essence or extract. Whisk the egg white lightly and add to the pan. Return the pan to low heat and cook for 2 minutes, stirring constantly.

Lightly dust a board or work surface with icing sugar and turn out the paste. Cover with cling film and leave until cold.

Knead the paste for 2-3 minutes, or until it is completely smooth and free of cracks. Wrap in a plastic bag and store in a cool, dry place.

This uncooked marzipan is good for modelling.

250g (8oz/2cups) ground almonds
450g (1lb/4cups) sifted icing (confectioner's) sugar
2 egg whites lightly beaten

Sift the icing sugar into a bowl with the ground almonds.

Make a well in the centre and add the lightly beaten egg whites.

Stir together to form a firm paste. Knead until smooth.

11

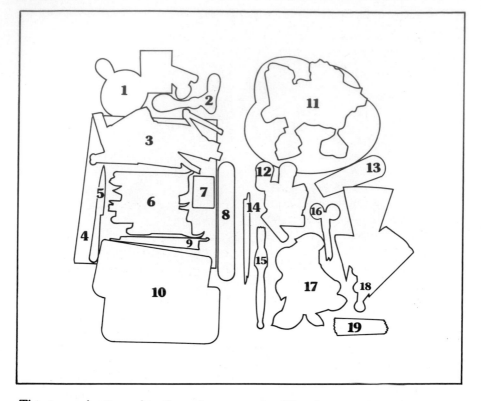

This is a selection of tools and equipment that can be used for marzipan work. Most are ordinary kitchen or household items, while the more unusual tools are available from cake decorating shops and specialist suppliers.

1 Wooden moulds
2 Buttons and small forms for embossing
3 Crimpers
4 Non-stick board
5 Sharp paring knife
6 Marzipan modelling tools
7 Glass-headed pins
8 Sugarpaste or marzipan smoothers
9 Crochet hooks
10 Cake boards
11 Biscuit cutters
12 Paste colours and petal dust
13 Nutmeg grater
14 Paintbrushes
15 Pastry brush
16 Scissors
17 Petal and leaf cutters
18 Piping bags and tubes
19 Cocktail sticks

WORKING WITH MARZIPAN

Marzipan is an easy medium to work with, and the same basic rules apply to all marzipan work. As in all sugarcraft, hygiene is important. Be sure that all work surfaces are clean and free from any dust or grease. Some of the new plastic nonstick boards and rolling pins make the work much easier. All equipment should be thoroughly cleaned as well. Always wash hands and clean fingernails before beginning work. Some cake decorators wear thin plastic surgical gloves to ensure cleanliness.

Colouring marzipan

Edible food colours are available in liquid and paste form, but paste colours are best for marzipan. Liquid colours may change the consistency of the marzipan.

To colour marzipan, cut off the amount necessary, place a small amount of paste colour in the centre, and knead until the colour is evenly distributed. To keep work surfaces and hands clean, the marzipan can be placed in a plastic bag and kneaded. Always start with a small amount of colour. If the marzipan is too pale, add a little more colour and knead again. If it is too dark, knead in another small piece of marzipan. If making several identical figures or colouring marzipan to cover a cake, try to colour enough at one time, as it is sometimes difficult to match colours.

Painting on marzipan

Painted colours can be used to add eyelashes and other features to modelled figures.

The marzipan must skin before painting, or the colours will sink in or run.

Never paint directly from the bottle of colour onto the marzipan. If using liquid colours, place some of the colour on greaseproof paper first. Dip the brush into the colour, wipe on the paper until there are no streaks, then paint on the marzipan. If using paste colours, put a few drops of water on the greaseproof paper, then add a small amount of paste colour and continue as before. If painting in several colours, be sure the first colour is dry before painting in the next one.

Rolling and cutting

When rolling out marzipan to make flat or cutout decorations, it is best to use one of the special plastic nonstick boards which are available. If working on a wooden or marble surface, dust it with a little icing sugar to prevent the marzipan from sticking. Do not dust with flour or cornflour, as these can cause fermentation. Use a small nonstick rolling pin, or a wooden rolling pin or piece of dowelling lightly dusted with icing sugar.

Marzipan can be cut with a sharp knife, scissors, or flower, biscuit, or aspic cutters. Take care not to mark the work surface. To remove cutouts from the board, carefully slip a small palette knife under the shape and lift it off slowly.

MARZIPANNING A CAKE FOR ROYAL ICING

Roll out the marzipan evenly. Brush the bottom of the cake with a purée of apricot jam and quickly turn over onto the marzipan. Cut round with a sharp knife.

Measure the circumference of the cake with a piece of string.

Brush the sides of the cake with a purée of apricot jam.

Roll out a long strip of marzipan and cut a little shorter than the circumference. Roll up the marzipan and unroll around the cake. Press round with a jar or tin.

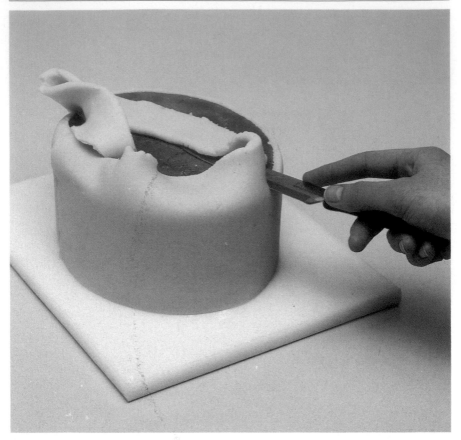

Use a sharp knife to trim off the
excess marzipan.

Place the board on top of the
marzipanned cake and turn over.

MARZIPANNING A CAKE FOR SUGARPASTE

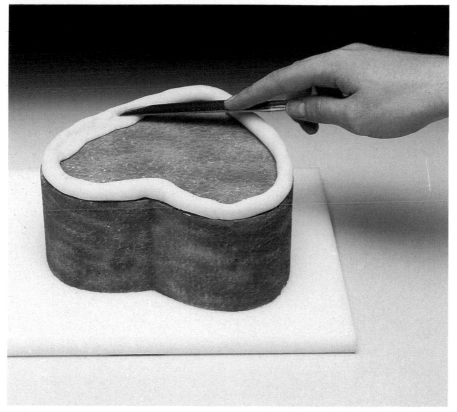

The cake is covered upside-down from the way it was baked — the base will be the top of the finished cake. Peel off the paper and fill in any holes in the sides or top with small pieces of marzipan. Smooth over to get a level surface.

Turn the cake upside-down. Brush the top and sides of the cake with a purée of apricot jam.

Dust the work surface with icing sugar, never flour or cornflour. Roll out the marzipan with a rolling pin. Prevent it from sticking by lifting and rotating it, but do not turn it over.

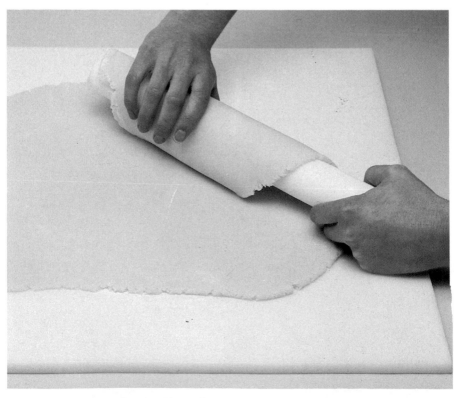

Carefully pick up the marzipan by draping it over the rolling pin.

Carefully drop the marzipan over
the cake, lifting the edges slightly
to help it fall without breaking.

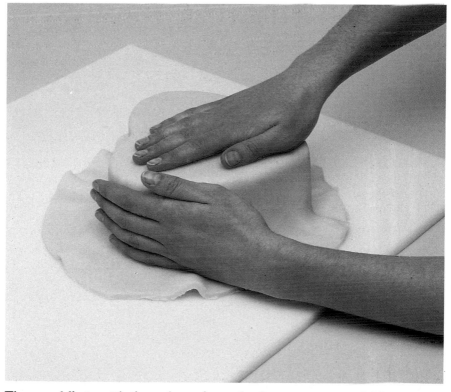

Then cuddle in with the palms of
your hands. Push up, don't pull
down or the marzipan may tear.
If the cake has corners, shape at
the corners first. Flare out from
the first corner to unfold any
pleats, then ease the marzipan
into the corner with an upward
movement of the hand.

21

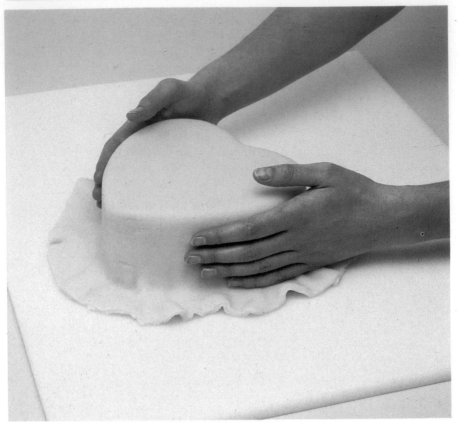

Use the palms of your hands to carefully smooth over the top of the cake.

Repair any tears by rubbing over them with the heel of the hand in a circular motion.

Cut off the surplus marzipan level with the bottom of the cake, using a sharp knife.

Use a smoother to push the cake to the edge of the surface. Lift by placing one hand under the cake and drop onto a prepared cake board. The marzipan must skin for a day or two before sugar-pasting.

HAND POSITIONS FOR FIGURE MODELLING

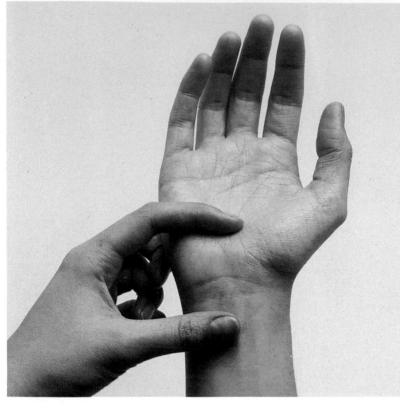

This is the position on the hand
where most of the figures are
modelled.

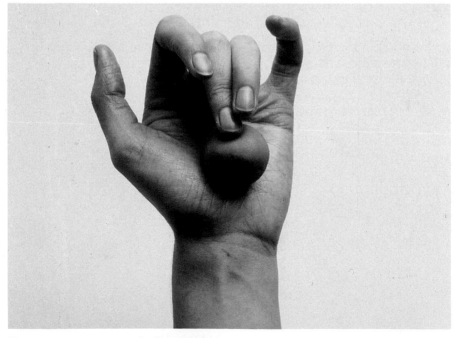

To form a point on a ball to make
a cone shape, place the ball at the
base of your palm.

The cone shape is formed at the base of the palms by moving your hands backwards and forwards.

To make an elongated cone, as for the elephant's trunk, have your hands as far apart as possible with your elbows tightly tucked by your hips. With the bases of your palms together, move your hands backwards and forwards.

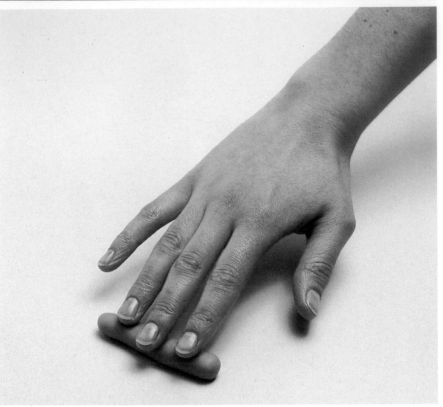

To make a sausage, first make a ball. Place the ball on the work surface and roll to a sausage shape using two fingers, then three fingers.

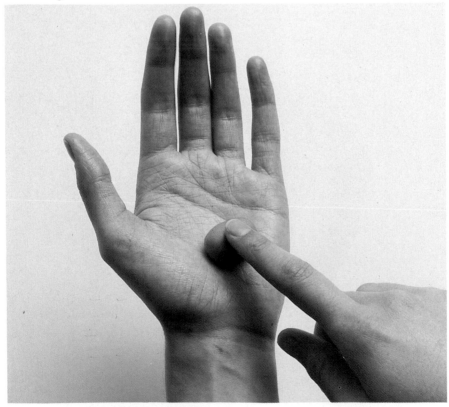

To make the butterbean shape, place a ball in the palm of your hands and use a finger to gently roll into a butterbean.

To make indentations for the eye sockets, hold the head in one hand and the ball tool in the other hand. Press the ball tool in firmly.

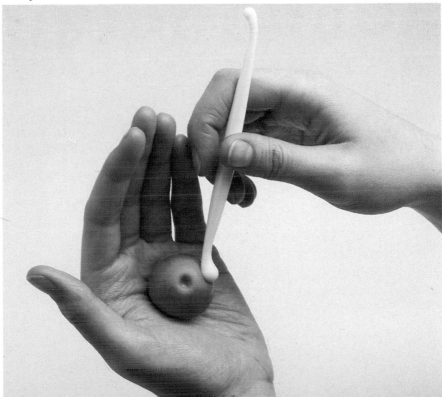

Move the handle of the ball tool upwards and remove.

RAINBOW CAKE

CRIMPER WORK

Crimper tools, sometimes called nippers, come in a combination of different shapes and widths. The most commonly used ones are 10mm (⅜in) wide and come in nine shapes: straight, curve, oval, vee, diamond, scallop, double scallop, heart and holly. The shapes can be used on their own or combined to make a great number of different patterns.

Crimper work must be done on fresh marzipan, or marzipan which has just skinned. The crimpers must be clean and dry. Dust them with a little icing sugar to prevent sticking. Adjust the crimpers to the right aperture, which depends on the size of the design, and hold with an elastic band. The wider the aperture, the more ridged effect will result when the crimpers are closed. Adjust the aperture by sliding the elastic band higher or lower along the crimper.

To make a crimper design, insert the crimpers into the marzipan, pinch together, release and move. If you forget to release the crimpers, a section of the marzipan will be torn.

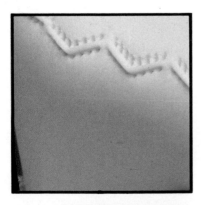

Details of crimper work showing designs on the edge of a cake and a marzipan basket crimped to resemble weaving.

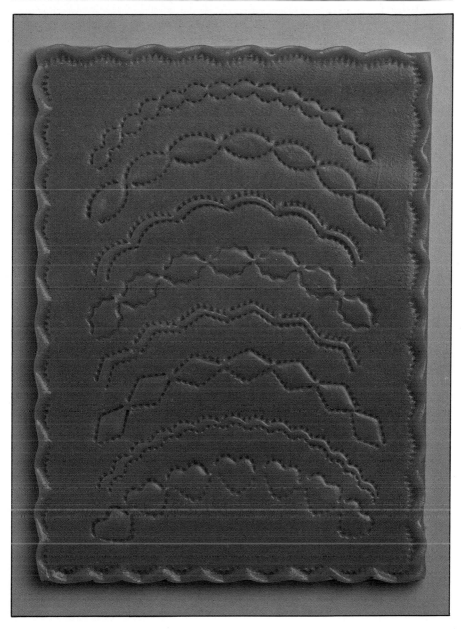

Crimpers and designs made with crimpers on marzipan.

MARQUETRY

Colourful marzipan marquetry can be used to make flat cutout decorations, like this clown, or as clothing for marzipan models. Colour the same amount of paste for each stripe, put them side by side and roll out thinly using spacers. Cut diagonally in strips and move each strip up one colour at a time to make the pattern. Re-roll to join into a sheet.

To make the flat clown, trace the photograph to make cardboard templates, then cut out from thinly rolled marzipan. Make a large square marquetry section and cut out the body using the template. Use the clown on top of a plainly iced cake, or place on a thin cake board.

To make the flat Christmas stockings, use marquetry and inlay marzipan. Trace the photograph to make a cardboard template. Make sections of marquetry and inlay as shown, then cut round the template using a sharp knife. Cut contrasting coloured strips for the tops and small round sections for the toes and heels. Mark with a nutmeg grater to get the effect of darning.

BISCUIT CUTTER DECORATIONS

Pastry, biscuit, cookie or aspic cutters can all be used to make flat marzipan decorations. Colour the marzipan as desired, roll it out thinly, and use the cutters to cut out the shapes. If necessary, dip the cutters in a little icing sugar to prevent sticking. Set the cutouts on a wooden board to dry, then decorate with piped royal icing or dragées, as wished. For individual party favours or place markers, pipe on names. To make pretty marzipan Christmas tree ornaments, make a small hole in the top of each cutout with a skewer and run a ribbon through.

CHRISTMAS CANDLES

Roll out bright red marzipan and use a ruler and a sharp knife to cut three different-sized candles. Place on a board or on top of an iced cake. To make the flames, cut a yellow marzipan circle using a round cutter, then cut the flame shape from the edge of the circle. Mark the centre with a thin red sausage and position over the candles. Pipe white icing for drippings. Arrange holly leaves around the candles, if wished.

SNOWMEN

Jolly snowmen make charming flat decorations to top a plain coloured-icing covered Christmas cake or winter birthday cake. Use the photographs to make templates, then cut out the snowmen from white marzipan which has been rolled thinly.

Mark features with a half-moon tool or a small ball tool, and position an orange oval nose. Make the hats from dark brown marzipan, using the photographs for templates. Make scarves, bow-tie and buttons from brightly coloured marzipan.

The snowmen's scarves are made from small sections of striped marzipan. Roll the stripes thinly using marzipan spacers, then cut to the required size. Use scissors to snip the fringes, cleaning the blades between each cut.

INLAY DESIGNS

Roll out blue marzipan and cut to fit a
thin cake board. Use a fish-shaped
biscuit cutter or draw a template to cut
out the fish from the plaque. Cut fish
from marquetry marzipan and carefully
place in the plaque. Roll over gently
with a rolling pin, and mark with a
grater. The cutout fish have inlay
stripes in contrasting colours.

MOSAIC WORK

Roll out the marzipan for the base very thinly and evenly. Use marzipan spacers or two pieces of wood of the same depth by the sides of the rolling pin. Roll out and cut the top decorations. Place the top decoration on the base, then go over it again so that it goes into the base. To get different textures into the finished work, roll over it with a ribbed roller or a piece of flex wrapped round dowelling, or mark with a button, nutmeg grater or cheese grater.

A mosaic design based on diamonds.

Inlay design made using aspic cutters.

Inlay design made using two sizes of biscuit cutters.

Plan the design first and draw it out. Roll out the marzipan and cut the shapes using aspic cutters or cardboard templates.

Assemble the design following the pattern on a thin cake board or directly onto the cake. When finished, go over it gently with a rolling pin to make sure pieces adhere.

39

INLAY BEE

This design is based on circles. Use round cutters to cut the body and head from yellow marzipan.

Roll out black marzipan and cut a circle using the same cutters as for the body. Cut two strips and position on the body. Trim and go over gently with a rolling pin to fix to the body. Cut small black circles for eyes.

Cut a white circle, then cut in half and shape for the wings. Assemble the bee as shown and trim with marzipan. Position on a thin cake board or place on top of a cake.

MARBLED MARQUETRY

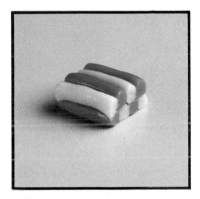

Make four sausages of each colour marzipan and put together alternately. Roll together to make a single fat sausage.

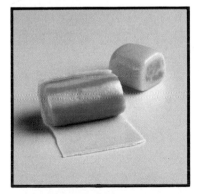

Roll out a thin strip of coloured marzipan and wrap around the marbled sausage. Roll again. If making the quilt for the cake, make several sausages in different sizes.

Cut the sausages in thin sections and place together to make a large section of marbled marquetry. Roll over with a rolling pin very lightly to make the sections stick together. To cover a cake, lift on a rolling pin very carefully and gently place over the cake.

PIGS IN BED

CUTOUT CHRISTMAS DECORATIONS

Trace the photograph and make cardboard templates. Roll out yellow marzipan and cut the two pieces for the body. Mark the lines with the back of a knife and make indentations for the buttons. The hair is a tapered sausage turned up at the ends.

Use a fluted round cutter for the wings. Cut out a triangle and mark with a knife. For the halo, make a ring and flatten slightly.

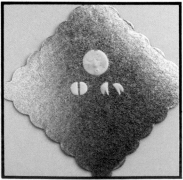

Cut a circle of pink marzipan for the head. Mark the eyes with a half-moon tool. The nose is a pink ball. Position another pink ball for the mouth, insert a cocktail stick, and rock up and down. Cut a smaller pink circle for the hands, cut in half, then cut out a small triangle to represent the fingers and thumb. Assemble the angel on a thin cake board or on top of a cake.

These decorations are
very simple to make and
do not need templates.
The bodies are equilateral
triangles, and the arms
are smaller triangles. The
other pieces are all based
on sections cut from
circles.

For the Father Christmas, cut a red,
pink and white circle using the same
round cutter. Cut sections from the
circles as shown for the hat, face and
beard.

DECORATIONS MADE WITH MOULDS

Attractive and easy-to-make decorations can be created from purchased metal or plastic confectionery moulds, wooden biscuit or cake moulds, or butter moulds. The technique for all these moulds is the same. Dust the mould with icing sugar. White or coloured marzipan is pressed into the mould, turned out carefully, and allowed to harden. It can then be painted.

Pretty marzipan Christmas tree ornaments can be made from traditional wooden biscuit moulds. Dust the moulds with icing sugar, press in white marzipan, then carefully smooth down to create an even level in the mould. Turn out, allow to skin, then paint as wished. To hang the decorations, carefully make a hole near the top while the marzipan is soft. Thread a ribbon through when dry.

An owl plaque made from a wooden cake mould. Dust the mould with icing sugar, press in the marzipan, then turn over onto a wooden board to smooth the bottom. Cut round the mould with a sharp knife to make the plaque. Turn out and allow to skin before painting in the details.

These party favours were made from daisy and swan butter moulds. Lightly dust the moulds with icing sugar before pressing in the marzipan. Colour each one differently to make individual party favours.

Colourful and unusual miniature decorations can be made from embossed, patterned and different-shaped buttons dusted with icing sugar. Simply press the button into rolled out marzipan, cut out with a sharp knife, and colour as wished.

Two different ways of using a plastic confectionery mould. The baby can either be left on a marzipan plaque, or carefully cut out with a sharp knife.

The fruit in this crystal
bowl are three-quarter
models of life-sized ones.
To assemble the arrange-
ment, be sure that all the
fruit is thoroughly dry,
then pile into an attractive
display. Use melted
chocolate to hold them
together, if necessary.

MARZIPAN FRUIT

Realistic models of every fruit and vegetable in the garden can be made from marzipan. Miniature models can be used to decorate cakes or boxes for attractive gifts, while larger models, up to life-sized, make lovely table decorations.

When modelling fruit and vegetables, try to work with the natural one in front of you to get the correct shape and colour. Marzipan models can be any size, so long as all the fruit or vegetables to be used in an arrangement are of the same proportions.

Grapes: Colour the marzipan either raspberry or pale green. For each grape, make a ball, then use a finger to roll it into a shape between a ball and a cone. Make several and arrange on a marzipan triangle base. Build up the grapes in layers to make a realistic bunch. Make a pale brown stalk, lift out a grape at the end, position the stalk and press in the grape.

Apple: Make a pale green ball, and make indentations in the top and bottom with the end of a paintbrush. Use the back of a knife to make a small cross in the top and bottom. Cut a clove in two and use one piece for the stem and the other for the calyx. Paint in the red markings.

Satsuma or clementine: Make an orange ball with an indentation at the top for the stem. Press the ball with a nutmeg grater to get the mottled effect. Use a clove for the stalk, or make three tiny brown tapered sausages and press in with a cocktail stick.

Orange: Make a larger ball, either round or slightly oval. Mark with a grater, indent with a ball tool and mark a star shape with the back of a knife.

50

This arrangement of miniature marzipan fruit could be used on top of a cake, or as a small table decoration or place marker. The fruits average about 2-2.5cm (¾-1in) in diameter. Arrange them in a marzipan basket decorated with crimper work to resemble weaving.

Lemon: Make a fat yellow sausage, then use a finger and thumb to gently stroke up one end. Mark the skin with a grater. Colour the other end with green food colouring or petal dust, then add a stalk.

Pear: Colour the marzipan either pale green or yellow. Make a ball, then make it into a pear shape by rolling gently between the heels of your hands. Make an indentation in the top. For the stalk, make a small, tapered brown sausage.

Grapefruit: Make a yellow ball, then flatten the top. Indent with a ball tool. Use the back of a knife to mark a star, then place a pale brown marzipan ball in the indentation. Mark the skin with a grater.

Peach: Make a ball of pale peach coloured marzipan. Use the back of a knife to mark a line down one side. Use cotton wool to apply pale pink colour on either side of the line. When the colour is dry, brush on the bloom with cotton wool dipped in cornflour.

Banana: Colour the marzipan yellow with a touch of brown and make a sausage with slightly tapered ends. Bend towards you, then shape the sides with the back of a knife. Colour the ends with dark brown food colouring and touch with a little green. Paint in the streaks and a few brown marks.

WHEELBARROW WITH VEGETABLES

To make the wheelbarrow, colour the marzipan light brown and roll out to about 5mm (¼in) thickness. Use the templates on the facing page to cut out the pieces. Assemble the wheelbarrow with melted chocolate, and coat the bottom with melted chocolate for extra strength.

Cut the wheel from marzipan and mark with the end of a spool or reel from sewing thread, or with something similar, like an embossed button. Attach with melted chocolate.

When the wheelbarrow is dry, fill with tiny marzipan models of vegetables — carrots, cauliflower, sprouts, onions, mushrooms, potatoes.

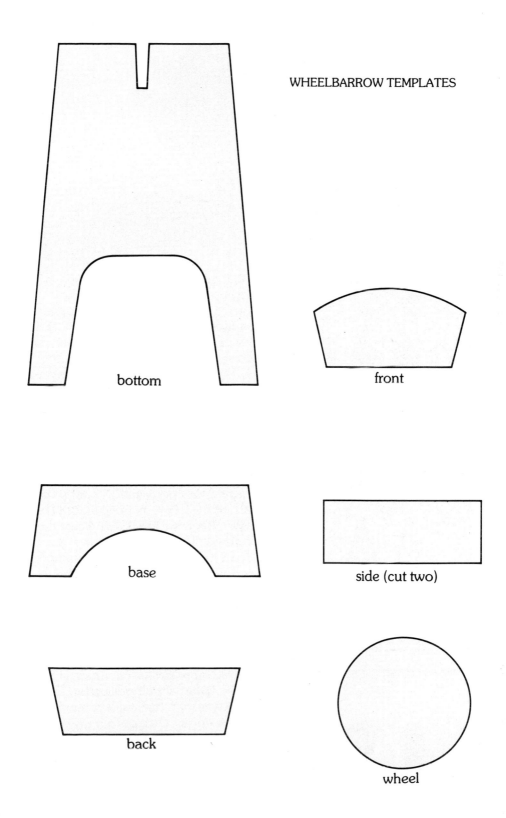

WHEELBARROW TEMPLATES

bottom

front

base

side (cut two)

back

wheel

ROSE

For the stand, make a cone with red marzipan. One-third of the way up, indent by gently rolling between the outside of your little fingers.

Roll out the marzipan very thinly and cut with a rose petal cutter. Soften the petals with a ball tool. Position the first petal on the cone as shown. Place the second petal opposite the first. Place three more petals interlocking using the edge of the second petal as the centre line of the third petal. At this stage it is called a half rose.

If adding more petals, cut them with the next larger-sized petal cutter. Fix them lower than the first layer and curl back the edges. Cut green marzipan leaves using a leaf cutter or a template.

CHRISTMAS ROSE

Roll white marzipan very thinly and cut out five petals using a rose petal cutter.

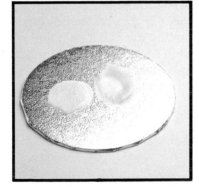

Use a ball tool to cup and flute each petal slightly. Attach the petals so that they overlap slightly.

Put a spot of thick royal icing in the centre and attach yellow stamens. To make the candle holder, position the Christmas roses on a small cake board and place a red candle in the centre. Use sugarpaste or royal icing to hold the candle.

55

POPPY AND BUTTERCUP

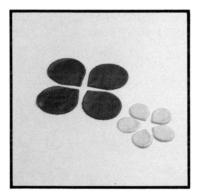

For the poppy, cut four red petals with a rose petal cutter. Cut five yellow petals for the buttercup using the smallest petal cutter.

Use a ball tool to flute and cup the poppy petals. Gently cup the buttercup petals by putting the ball tool in the centre of each one.

To make the centre of the poppy, make a small black cone and attach a black circle marked with lines. Press in short black stamens and fix with royal icing. Assemble the buttercup by overlapping the petals slightly and attaching with royal icing. Press the stamens into the centre.

SWEET PEAS

Sweet peas can be pink, mauve, red or white. For the centre, make a cone and flatten one edge slightly. Using a rose petal cutter, cut a petal. Place the cone in the centre and carefully fold the petal in half.

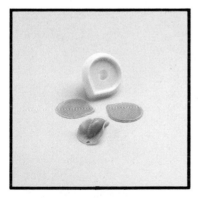

Cut two petals using the next larger-sized cutter. Flute with a ball tool on palm of hand or cocktail stick on a board. Attach the first petal to the base of the cone, bringing the sides of the petal forward.

Curve the second petal back and attach at the base of the previous layer.

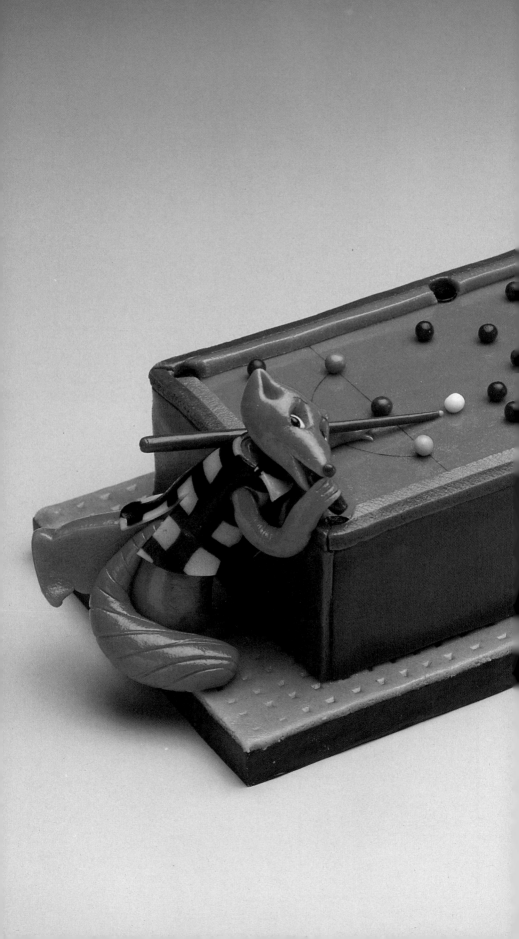

CREATING CHARACTERS

Each marzipan figure should have its own individual personality, with a different story to tell. By changing the facial expressions, particularly the eyes, and changing the colour and style of the hair, each figure becomes a unique character. If piping the eyes, always indent with a ball tool first. The noses are pink balls. The faces shown here can be adapted for both cutout and free-standing marzipan figures.

Pipe one eye and mark the closed eye with a half-moon marzipan tool. Use the same tool to mark the mouth. Cut black marzipan for the hair and place a tiny ball on top of the head for a bun.

For a surprised expression pipe both eyes with the pupils looking up. Position a small pink ball for the mouth, then place cocktail stick inside and rock up and down. Make a red sausage and snip hair.

Pipe both eyes with pupils looking in the same direction. Position a small pink ball for the mouth, then place cocktail stick inside and rock it side to side. Shape yellow marzipan hair and mark with the back of a knife.

Pipe one eye and mark the other and the mouth with a half-moon tool. Shape red marzipan and mark the curls with the back of a knife.

A simple face marked with the half-moon tool. Make sausages for plaits, snip ends and make tapered sausages for bows.

Pipe eyes with pupils facing in the same direction. Position a small pink ball for the mouth, then place a cocktail stick inside and rock it up and down. Make a red tapered sausage and bend for the curls.

Pipe eyes with pupils facing inwards. Position balls for ears, indent with ball tool and marzipan strips for earrings. Coloured tapered sausages make the 'mohawk' haircut.

HATS

Another way of creating different characters from basic marzipan figures is to give them different hats. Make the hats from coloured marzipan or modelling paste.

For a Santa Claus hat, make a cone from red marzipan, elongate the end and turn it down. Cut the white fur from rolled-out marzipan or sugarpaste using a fluted cutter. Position the flattened end of the cone, turn up the edges of the fur and mark with a cocktail stick or small ball tool. Put a white ball of fur on the tip.

Make flat caps by making a round ball and flattening it. Place smaller flattened balls on top. Make a tiny ball for the centre.

Make a round ball and flatten. Make a ball for the top, flatten it slightly, and place on the circle. Mark with a knife or decorate with tiny flowers.

For top hats, colour the marzipan black. Make a round ball and flatten. Make a sausage for the top.

Make a small round ball and flatten. Make a ball from the same colour and place on top. Mark the centre with the back of a knife. The brim can either be left down or turned up at the sides. Add a small marzipan feather for a huntsman's cap.

To make these coloured caps, first make two identical balls using different coloured marzipan. Cut them in half, then into quarters. Reassemble as shown and make into a ball. Place on a coloured circle and add a tiny ball on top.

For these feminine hats, make small round balls and flatten. Place in a plastic bag and press out the edges to make them very thin. Place a ball or slightly flattened ball on top, and decorate with thinly rolled marzipan ribbons and tiny flowers.

MARZIPAN FIGURES

Figure modelling is one of the most delightful of all the sugarcraft skills. All of the charming animals and human figures here and on the following pages are made using the basic shapes and hand positions on pages 24 to 27. Each marzipan model should be an individual character. Use the different facial expressions and hats to create the humorous personalities and interesting characters.

MOUSE

For the body and head, take 5g (1/6oz) white marzipan. Make a ball in the palm of the hand, then roll into a cone.

Make indentations for eyes. Attach a tiny pink marzipan ball for the nose and press up with a finger. Make two small white balls for ears, attach and press shape with ball tool. Pipe eyes.

For the tail, take a small piece of brown marzipan and roll into a long, very thin sausage tapering at both ends. Attach to mouse and curl in an S-shape over the back.

HEDGEHOG

For the body and head, take 5g (⅙oz) brown marzipan. Make a ball in the palm of the hand, then roll into a cone.

Use a pair of small, sharp, pointed scissors to make the spikes. Start from the back of the body, snip and push up with scissors for each spike. Clean scissors between each cut to prevent tearing the marzipan. For the next row cut in between the spikes of the first row.

Attach a tiny pink ball for the nose and press up with a finger. Make indentations for eyes and pipe.

DUCK

For the body, take 10g (⅓oz) white marzipan and roll into a cone in the base of the hands. Mark tail feathers with a knife and turn up. Make an indentation for the head to rest in.

Head is a 4g (⅐oz) ball. Make indentations for the eyes with a ball tool. Make a tiny orange carrot for the beak and attach to the head with the fat side up.

Make a 2g (1/15oz) orange sausage for the feet and bend into a V-shape. Flatten the ends and mark for the webbed feet. Attach under body. Pipe eyes.

CHICK

For the body, make a ball with 15g (½oz) yellow marzipan. Indent the centre for the head to sit.

Head is a 4g (⅐oz) ball. Make indentations for the eyes.

Roll out red marzipan into a flat strip. Cut a diagonal from the end, then cut diagonally for a diamond-shaped beak. Press a cocktail stick into the centre of the diamond and press in for the mouth. Cut triangles from strip and attach to top of head for comb. Pipe eyes.

FROG

A simple way of making the bride's veil is to cut a petal shape from thinly rolled sugarpaste or marzipan and then mark the lace pattern by pressing in with a decorative button or similar item. The groom's jacket can be made by cutting a circle from black marzipan. Cut a smaller circle for the neck, mark with a knife, and wrap the jacket around the figure.

For the body, make a cone with 20g (⅔oz) green marzipan. Flatten top slightly for head.

For the legs, make a sausage with 5g (⅙oz). With the outside of the little finger, indent to show thigh and ankle. Cut lengthwise. Flatten one end of each leg to form feet and cut for toes. Attach legs to body and bend into position. Place a tiny ball of marzipan on each toe. Use 2g (1/15oz) marzipan for both arms and make as for legs.

For the head, make a cone with 5g (⅙oz). Flatten the end for the mouth and cut with a sharp, pointed knife. Place point of knife in mouth and press down to open it. Squeeze sides to make a smile, then use small end of ball tool to press in the sides. Use finger and thumb to press and stroke top of head to form eyebrows. Make indentations with a ball tool for eye sockets and pipe eyes. Make indentations for nostrils with a cocktail stick. For the tongue, make a cone from red marzipan, flatten it, mark a line down the centre with a cocktail stick, and position tongue in mouth.

PIG

For the head and body, make a cone with 20g (2/3oz) pink marzipan. Indent with the outside of the little finger for the snout.

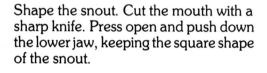

Shape the snout. Cut the mouth with a sharp knife. Press open and push down the lower jaw, keeping the square shape of the snout.

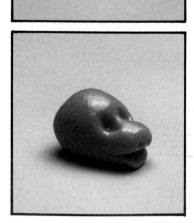

Make indentations for the nostrils with a cocktail stick. Use a ball tool to make indentations for the eye sockets.

Make two small, flat cones for the ears. Attach the fat end to the head and bend the tip forward.

The tail is a long, thin sausage. Taper the end. Attach to the body, squiggle, and leave the point sticking up.

Make four small balls for the feet and position under the body. Pipe eyes and place a flat red cone in the mouth for the tongue.

SITTING PIG

For the head, make an 8g (¼oz) cone. Indent with the outside of the little finger and rock the finger to make the snout. Indent with a ball tool for the eyes. Cut mouth and mark nostrils with a cocktail stick. The ears are two small flattened cones. Attach fat side to head and turn up.

Make a fat sausage with 15g (½oz) for the body. Position head and pipe eyes. Make a thin, tapered sausage for the tail, attach and curl round.

Legs and arms are the same. Make a sausage for each pair, indent for trotters, cut lengthwise, flatten and cut out a V-shape. Paint tips of trotters with black food colouring and attach legs and arms to body.

RABBIT

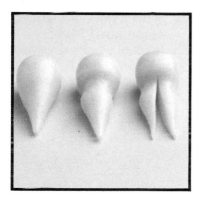

For the head, make an 8g (¼oz) cone. Indent with the outside of the little finger for the base of the ears, then cut through the cone to make two ears. Indent with a ball tool.

Indent eye sockets with a ball tool. Gently press out the sides of the face, then snip with sharp scissors for the whiskers. Nose is a tiny pink marzipan ball. To make the mouth, roll out a small piece of sugarpaste and cut a small rectangle. Cut to make two teeth. Leave to harden and press into the mouth on the face. Pipe eyes.

The body is a 20g (⅔oz) cone. Make an indentation at the top for the head to rest in. Make a small sausage for each hand, taper, bend forward and mark paws with the back of a knife. Make two small balls for the feet, flatten them slightly and place under the body. Make a ball for the tail and snip with scissors to make it look fluffy.

DOG

For the body, make a sausage with 15g (½oz) white marzipan. Make several small circles of black marzipan and press on body for spots. Roll again.

Place a black half-circle in position for each paw. Make cuts for front and back legs. Bend sausage and separate the legs.

Make a 5g (⅙oz) cone for the head. Indent with a ball tool for the eyes. Make a tiny black marzipan oval for the nose, position and turn up slightly.

Place a small oval of black marzipan in one of the eye sockets. Indent again with the ball tool, then pipe the eyes.

Make two small black cones for the ears. Flatten, then attach the pointed end to the side of the head.

Make another black cone for the tail, flatten it and attach the rounded end to the body. Position the head.

CAT

For the body, make a cone with 15g (½oz) white marzipan. Attach a long, tapered sausage for the tail.

Make a 5g (⅙oz) ball for the head. Gently pinch up ears and indent with a ball tool. Make indentations for eyes and pipe. Mark whiskers with a knife. Add small nose and mouth of pink marzipan.

For a different face, use thumb and forefinger to gently stroke out sides of face, then snip with sharp scissors for whiskers. Finish as for other face and attach head to body.

CROCODILE

Take 20g (⅔oz) dark green marzipan, make a sausage for the head and body, and then elongate one end for the tail. Make the tail pointed by squeezing with finger and thumb. Cut with scissors to make scales. Use a ball tool to press along the sides of the body, then squeeze with fingers to make the ridges of the back.

Cut the mouth with a knife and press open. Make tiny white cones for the teeth and press into mouth with a cocktail stick. Make a red flattened cone and place in mouth for tongue. Make holes for nostrils with a cocktail stick and pipe. Make two small green balls for the eyes. Position, then make indentations with a ball tool. Place small white balls in sockets, then tiny brown balls for pupils.

Make two small sausages, indent for legs. Cut in half lengthwise, mark the feet and press out with fingers. Attach to sides of body.

FOX

For the body, make an elongated cone with 15g (½oz) orange marzipan. Cut pointed end of cone down the centre and bend legs over to shape. Mark paws with the back of a knife. Point the front end slightly for the neck.

Tail is a 5g (⅙oz) sausage with a tapered end. Curve, then mark with the back of a knife. Attach to body.

Make a 5g (⅙oz) cone for the head. Stroke up ears, then indent them and the eye sockets with a ball tool. Turn up the end of the nose and attach a small brown marzipan oval. Cut mouth. Use the end of a paintbrush to make a hole in the bottom of the head and place on neck end of body. Pipe eyes.

DRAGON

For the body, make a 25g (¾oz) green cone and flatten top slightly. Use a half-moon marzipan tool to make indentations for scales.

Tail is a 10g (⅓oz) sausage. Press finger in for thick end and place under body. Mark scales and position red triangles down centre.

Make a 5g (⅙oz) sausage for the legs. Make indentations, cut in half lengthwise and position on body. Mark scales. Feet are small white cones. Make three cuts for claws, shape with finger and thumb and position. Make a 3g (¹⁄₁₀oz) cone for the arms. Cut in half, mark scales and position. Cut and shape white claws as for feet.

Use a biscuit or calyx cutter to make a star-shaped collar. Cut down the points to look like flames. Cut triangular wings from green marzipan. Mark scales and cut sides with scissors. Curve and attach to back.

Make a 10g (⅓oz) long cone for head. Indent with a finger for face, for eye sockets with a ball tool. Mark scales. Eyes are small balls of yellow marzipan with smaller red balls for pupils. Make tiny red balls for nostrils and indent with cocktail stick. Cut the mouth and open it wide. Flatten white cone for inside, with tiny cones for teeth. Make a red cone for the tongue. Press down with a cocktail stick inside mouth.

For each ear make a green cone and press together with a smaller red cone. Hollow with a ball tool and press into ear sockets. Attach head to body and position red triangles down the back of the dragon.

TEDDY BEAR

Colour the marzipan yellow with a touch of brown. For the body, make a cone with 20g (⅔oz) and flatten the top slightly for the head.

For the legs, make a sausage with 5g (⅙oz). Indent with the little finger. Cut in half lengthwise, turn up the feet and attach legs to body. Mark claws with the back of a knife. Use 2g (¹⁄₁₅oz) for both arms and make as for legs.

For the head, make a cone with 10g (⅓oz) marzipan. Cut mouth with a sharp knife, place the knife point inside and press down to open. Squeeze sides of the mouth to make a smile. Make indentations with a ball tool for the eye sockets. For the ears, make tiny balls and attach. Place a finger behind each ear and indent with a ball tool. Make a tiny brown oval and position on the end of the nose. Pipe eyes.

STANDING MOUSE

Make a 5g (⅙oz) cone for the head and indent for eyes. The nose is a tiny pink ball. For the ears, make two tiny balls, position on the head, and indent with a ball tool. Alternatively, indent before placing on head, position pink balls for the inside, then position and indent again.   Pipe eyes.

Make a 15g (½oz) cone for the body. The feet are small flattened cones. Snip for toes, then place under body.

Make a 1g (⅓₀oz) sausage for each arm. Taper the top end, then flatten the other end for the hand. Snip for fingers and place around body.

KOALA

The body is made from two cones. Make a 25g (¾oz) brown cone, and use your finger to make an indentation in the centre. Press in a 5g (⅙oz) white cone and roll them together. Flatten the top to take the head.

Make a 10g (⅓oz) sausage for the legs. Indent for feet, cut lengthwise, press up feet, mark paws and attach. Make a 5g (⅙oz) sausage for the arms, indent for paws, cut lengthwise, mark claws and position.

Make a 10g (⅓oz) ball for the head. Squeeze and stroke the sides, then snip with scissors for the fur. Make two small brown balls for the ears. Flatten then indent them and place smaller white balls in the indentation. Attach, then indent again. Squeeze the outside edges, then snip with scissors. Eyes are tiny black marzipan balls; nose is a black oval.

MOUSE WEDDING CAKE

KANGAROO

For the body, make a cone with 20g (⅔oz) light brown marzipan. Roll between the palms of the hands to make the tail. Curve the top end for the neck and flatten slightly.

Make a 5g (⅙oz) cone for the legs. Use the outside of your little finger to indent for the muscle. Cut lengthwise, flatten the ends and cut the feet. Bend and attach to the body.

Make the apron, collar and hat from pink marzipan. For the apron, cut with a fluted cutter, then cut a piece for the top with a rounded cutter. Use a ball tool or a cocktail stick to make the pattern. For the ties, make long, thin sausages and make a bow in the back. Use a small fluted cutter for the collar and place on the neck.

Make a 5g (⅙oz) cone for the head. Indent the eye sockets with a ball tool. Cut the mouth with a sharp knife and open slightly. Attach a ball of dark brown marzipan for the nose. Pipe the eyes. For the ears, make two cones, indent with a ball tool and attach.

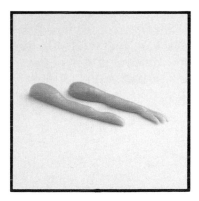

Make the baby's head exactly as for the mother's, starting with a 2g (1/15oz) cone.

Make the mother's arms with a 2g (1/15oz) cone. Cut lengthwise, flatten the ends, cut the hands, and attach to the body. Cradle the baby's head in the mother's arms.

PANDA

Make a 25g (¾oz) cone of white marzipan for the body and flatten the top to take the head.

Make a 10g (⅓oz) black sausage for the legs. Indent twice for the muscle and the paws. Cut lengthwise, turn up the paws and attach legs to the body. Make a black sausage with 5g (⅙oz) for the arms and make as for the legs.

The head is a 10g (⅓oz) white cone. The eyes are tiny black rectangles cut from rolled marzipan. Attach a black oval nose. The ears are small black balls. Indent with a ball tool after attaching.

ELEPHANT

Make a fat sausage with 50g (1⅔oz) of pink marzipan for the body and legs. Cut at both ends and separate for the legs. Bend to shape. Make indentations with a ball tool for the toes. Attach a small, flattened cone for the tail.

For the head, make a 30g (1oz) cone and elongate for the trunk. Bend the trunk up. Cut the mouth with a knife, and indent the eye sockets with a ball tool.

For the ears, make two balls. Make indentations with your finger, leaving a ridge around the top edge, and attach the ears to the sides of the head. Pipe the eyes.

TORTOISE

Colour the marzipan marbled brown. Make a 5g (⅙oz) sausage for the body and taper the end for the tail. Cut the mouth with a knife and mark nostrils and indent for eyes with a cocktail stick. Pipe eyes.

Make four tiny balls for feet and attach to body. Mark paws with a cocktail stick.

Make a 10g (⅓oz) ball for the shell. Press out edges between finger and thumb, then mark with the back of a knife. Mark circles on back by pressing in the wide end of a piping tube. Place shell on body and turn up tail.

FISH

For the body, make a 5g (⅙oz) yellow sausage and taper it slightly at one end. Make a small orange sausage, wrap it around the body and roll them together. Mark back with knife. Make an indentation with a cocktail stick at either side of the body and one at the end.

Make a green ball for the face. Flatten it and cut a triangle from the top. Place on body and indent for the eyes. Position a small yellow ball for the mouth, then place a cocktail stick inside and rock it up and down to make mouth open.

Make green flattened cones for the fins. Snip with scissors and place thin ends in indentations at sides. Make a larger cone for the tail, flatten, snip and position. Pipe eyes.

REINDEER FATHER CHRISTMAS

Make the reindeer head as shown here. Make the body from red marzipan. The fur trimmings and beard are made from sugarpaste.

REINDEER

For the head, make an elongated cone with 20g (⅔oz) brown marzipan. Pinch out the nose with your fingers, then stroke at the thick end to make the neck. Indent ear holes with the end of a paintbrush. Use a ball tool to make the eye sockets and mark the nostrils with a cocktail stick. Cut the mouth with a sharp knife, then press gently to open.

Nose and tongue are red marzipan. Make cones for the ears, indent with a cocktail stick and fit the wide ends into the holes. Pipe eyes. Use a knife to cut the pointed end to make two antlers. Spread out and twist. Place the head flat on the board, flatten the antlers and shape them. Cut horns around the edge with a knife.

The body and the legs are a long 45g (1½oz) sausage. Indent the ends for the hooves. With a knife, cut two-thirds of the way along each end for the legs. Bend the body to shape. Snip at the back with scissors for the tail.

KEEP-FIT CLASS

SANTA CLAUS

Make a 15g (½oz) pink ball for the head, and make indentations for the eyes, nose and mouth. Press in two red circles for the cheeks. Press in a pink ball for the nose.

Make the beard and moustache from white sugarpaste. Cut the beard using a fluted cutter, then cut out a section with a round cutter. Mark with a knife and wrap around the face. Make a white sausage for the moustache and taper the ends. Position on the face, then add the mouth to hold them in place. The mouth is a pink ball. Insert a cocktail stick and rock up and down to make the mouth open.

For the body, make a red 50g (1⅔oz) cone. Cut out the white base, place under body, then press into sides with a ball tool. Add the buttons.

Arms are a 5g (⅙oz) red sausage. Taper ends, cut in half, add a small white circle for the cuff, and indent for hands. Hands are flattened pink cones. Cut fingers and insert in cuffs. Attach arms to body.

Make a 10g (⅓oz) red cone for the hat. Cut the white base using a fluted cutter, place under the hat and press up around the sides with a ball tool. Add a white bobble. Pipe hair with royal icing, then put hat on top. Pipe eyes and eyebrows.

The sack is made from brown marzipan, following the instructions on page 122. Make miniature animals, such as the tiny frog and teddy, for toys.

CHOIR GIRL

Make a 5g (⅙oz) pink ball for the head and place it on a cocktail stick. Paint the face and hair with food colouring. Place the cocktail stick in polystyrene and leave until dry.

The body is a 20g (⅔oz) red cone. The arms are a 5g (⅙oz) red sausage. Taper the ends, cut in half, make indentations for the hands, and position on the body. Push tiny pink balls in the sleeves for hands and mark fingers with a knife.

For the hat, roll out and cut a black square. Put a tiny ball in the centre, then two little sausages for tassles. Remove cocktail stick and attach head with royal icing. Place the hat on the head. Decorate with piped royal icing.

ANGEL

Make a 5g (⅙oz) pink ball for the head and place it on a cocktail stick. Paint the face and hair with food colouring. Place the cocktail stick in polystyrene and leave until dry.

The body is a 20g (⅔oz) yellow cone. The arms are a 5g (⅙oz) yellow sausage. Taper the ends, cut in half, make indentations for the hands and position on the body. Push tiny pink balls in the sleeves for hands and mark fingers with a knife. To make the wings, roll out white marzipan, cut with a fluted cutter, cut out a V-shaped section for the back, mark wings with a knife, and attach to the body.

For the crown, make a 1g (⅓₀oz) ball with dark yellow marzipan. Make an X with a knife, then lift the points to make a crown. Assemble the angel and pipe decorations with white royal icing.

GIRL

Make a 5g (⅙oz) pink ball for the head. Indent for the eyes, nose and mouth. The nose is a tiny cone. Make a ball for the mouth, position, put a cocktail stick in the centre and gently move up and down to open the mouth. For the long hair, make a sausage, taper the ends, position and snip. The fringe is a flat piece. Snip with scissors.

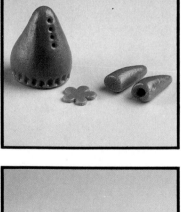

The body is a 25g (¾oz) mauve cone. The arms are a 5g (⅙oz) mauve sausage. Taper the ends, cut in half, make indentations for the hands, and position on the body. Push tiny pink balls in the sleeves for hands and mark fingers with a knife. Cut out the collar using a fluted cutter.

Assemble the figure and pipe eyes and decorations with royal icing.

BOY

Make a 5g (⅙oz) pink ball for the head. Indent for the eyes, nose and mouth. The nose is a tiny cone. Make a ball for the mouth, position, put a cocktail stick in the centre and gently rock from side to side to open the mouth. Position yellow marzipan hair and mark with a knife.

Make a 25g (¾oz) blue sausage and cone the top for the body. Cut three-quarters of the way down the centre for the trousers and mark the belt. Make two indentations for the buttons. Make the arms and hands exactly as for the Girl.

Make two green flattened cones for the shoes. Position, then assemble the figure and place on its back to dry. Royal ice the eyes and decorations.

BABY

Make a 15g (½oz) cone for the body.

For the head, make a 5g (⅙oz) ball. Indent across the middle using the outside of your little finger, and mark the eyes with a ball tool. The ears are a tiny tapered sausage. Cut in half, taper into a question mark shape, attach and leave to set. The white baby's mouth is cut using a sharp knife. For the black baby, make a sausage, position on the face, insert a cocktail stick and rock gently from side to side. Pipe eyes.

For the legs, make a 3g (¹⁄₁₀oz) sausage. Indent with the outside of your little finger. Cut down the centre. Pinch up for the heel and mark toes. Position on body. The arms are a 2g (¹⁄₁₅oz) sausage. Taper one end, then roll with finger to make elbow and wrist. Cut down the centre, flatten the end for the hand, then cut for the fingers and thumb. Bend and position on the body.

FISHERMAN

Make a 10g (⅓oz) pink ball for the head and made indentations for the eyes, nose and mouth. The nose is a pink ball. Make a small brown sausage for the moustache, taper the ends and position. Make a ball for the mouth, position, insert a cocktail stick and move gently up and down to open mouth. Ears are tiny pink balls. Position and indent. Add brown marzipan hair and mark with a knife. Pipe eyes.

The sweater is a 15g (½oz) green cone. Make a green sausage and position for the poloneck. Make a 5g (⅙oz) sausage for the arms. Taper and cut in half. Make two small pink cones for hands. Flatten the ends and cut fingers.

The trousers and boots are made in one piece. Take a 20g (⅔oz) yellow sausage and a 10g (⅓oz) black sausage and roll them together to make a long sausage. Cut three-quarters of the way down the middle to make the two legs and the seat. Bend to shape.

The fishing rod is a long, thin brown marzipan sausage. Leave to set very hard. Use sewing thread for the fishing line.

Marble brown and white marzipan and mould into the log. Assemble the figure on the log and place on a thin cake board, or on top of a cake.

The octopus is made from purple marzipan. Make a ball for the head and indent for the eyes. Press in a half-moon marzipan tool for the mouth. Pipe the eyes. Make eight long tapered sausages for the legs and arrange under the body.

CHARLADY

Make a 10g (⅓oz) pink ball for the head. Indent for the eyes, nose and mouth. The nose is a pink ball. Make a red ball for the mouth, position, and shape by inserting a cocktail stick and rocking from side to side. Add a cigarette made from marzipan or rice paper.

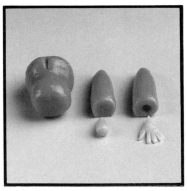

The blouse is a 10g (⅓oz) pink cone. Indent under the bust with the outside of your little finger, then mark the bust with a knife. Make a 5g (⅙oz) sausage for the arms, taper one end and cut in half. Indent the fat end and position pink flattened cones for hands. Cut the fingers.

Make a 15g (½oz) brown cone for the skirt and position the blouse on top. The slippers are pink flattened cones. Place under the body.

Roll out white marzipan and cut out the apron using the template. Put tiny pink balls on the apron and press in gently. Wrap around the body.

Cut a white triangle for the scarf and add red balls. Flatten and roll together. Cut a strip for the bow and place around the head.

The mop handle is a long brown marzipan sausage. Allow to harden thoroughly. Make a white ball for the mop and snip the ends. Make a 5g (⅙oz) brown cone and indent in the centre for the bucket. Add a small thin sausage for the handle. Make the mouse and place in the bucket.

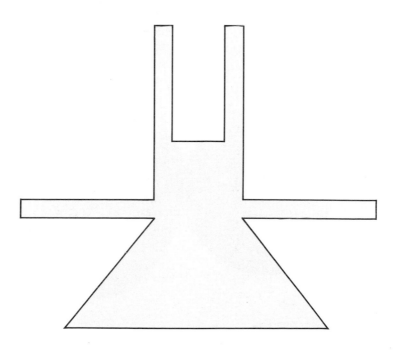

CLOWN

Make a 40g (1⅓oz) ball of white marzipan for the head. Make two small balls for the ears and press in with a ball tool. Take a yellow strip for the hair, snip ends and place around head. Press in a red ball for the nose and red circles for cheeks. Make a red sausage for the mouth. Indent eye sockets with a ball tool. Press crossed strips of dark blue marzipan in the sockets, then pipe eyes. Make red half-moon eyebrows.

The top of the body is a 50g (1⅔oz) ball. Position coloured rainbow stripes around the body. Braces are two mauve strips. The jacket is marquetry. Roll together and place around the body. To set, place on a small container so the jacket hangs down and leave overnight.

Make an orange strip for the lapels and collar. Attach to the side of the jacket, around the neck and down the other side. Make tiny red balls for buttons and cut indentations for buttonholes. For the flowers, flute thin coloured strips of marzipan with a cocktail stick and position for the buttonhole.

Make a 15g (½oz) sausage for the arms and wrap a marquetry section around it. Cut lengthwise and position both arms on body. Make holes in the sleeve ends for hands. For the hands, make flattened cones and cut fingers.

Make a 50g (1⅔oz) sausage for legs. Cut halfway down, part the legs and wrap marquetry around them. Leave a section uncovered at the top for the body to rest in. Leave on a piece of foam, but before it is completely dry put it under the body and press top of trousers over body.

Use 35g (1¼oz) orange marzipan for both boots. Make fat cones, indent them with a finger and place them under the trousers. Cut for the soles.

For the hat, make a multicoloured ball, flatten the base, then work in a plastic bag to make the sides floppy. Place a smaller ball on top and indent down the centre with a knife. Place on the clown's head.

HALLOWE'EN CAKE

VALENTINE CARD

Roll out red marzipan and cut out a heart using a large heart biscuit cutter or a template. Crimp the edges. Cut out the figures and the tiny hearts, and assemble the card with royal icing.

EASTER EGG BASKET

Make the basket by pressing pale brown marzipan into a basket mould, which has been dusted with icing sugar. The eggs are made from marbled marzipan. Roll into eggs. Decorate some of the eggs with tiny cut-out rabbits. Arrange in the basket.

CHRISTMAS CRACKERS

For each cracker, make a red marzipan sausage and mark each end with the back of a knife. To make the frills, first dip a cocktail stick in icing sugar and press in each end. Dip your thumb in icing sugar and thin the marzipan between your thumb and the cocktail stick, turning. Snip with scissors. The scissors must be cleaned between each cut or the marzipan may tear. Decorate with royal icing when skinned.

CHRISTMAS PIGS

To make these traditional Scandinavian and German Christmas favours, make pink marzipan pigs following the instructions on page 72. Purchase foil wrapped chocolate coins. To place in the pig's mouth, cut the mouth deeper than usual and press the coin inside. To put the coin in the pig's back, make an indentation with the back of a knife and press the coin in.

SANTA'S SACK

Make a cone from brown marzi-pan and flatten the base. Indent the top with a ball tool or with your finger, then gently stroke up the sides to make them thin and to open the sack. The opening should go about one-third of the way down the sack and be nearly as wide as the base. Fill with marzipan presents and tiny animals.

HALLOWE'EN IDEAS

Witch: Make a pale pink elongated cone with 5g (⅙oz) pale pink marzipan. Turn up the end to make a pointed chin. Indent for the eye sockets. Position a pale pink ball for the mouth. Insert a cocktail stick and rock it up and down to open the mouth. Make a small pink cone for the nose and hook downwards towards the chin. Make black tapered sausages for the hair and place on head. Make a black cone for the hat and decorate with different coloured stars and moons. Pipe eyes.

Jack-o-lantern: Make a round orange ball and flatten slightly. Mark the indentations with a round cutter. Make indentations for the eyes and a moon for the mouth. Make an indentation in the top and position a green cone for the stalk. Pipe eyes.

INSTRUCTIONS FOR CAKES

Cats on a cushion: Make an oval cake, then cut away part of the base and shape the top. Roll out brown marzipan, flute it and come up half-way from the base of the cake. Roll out more marzipan, gather, place over the top of the cake and come half-way down. Hide the join with a long sausage wrapped round the cake. Make indentations for the cats.

Rainbow cake: Marble sugarpaste with blue and position for the sky. The grass is green sugarpaste. The marzipan rainbow is a marquetry section. Make between spacers, or use two pieces of cardboard of the same height. Measure the sections and bend to shape. Attach with royal icing. The figures are made from biscuit cutters. Make flower cutter flowers and indent each flower on a sponge to get the three-dimensional effect. Attach with royal icing.

Pigs in bed: Cover a round cake with buttercream. The sheet is white sugarpaste. Make a yellow marzipan sausage and place round the cake for the bolster. Make indentations for the heads to rest. Make the pigs' heads and arms and place on the cake. Put marzipan sausages on the cake to represent bodies. Make the quilt following the instructions for marquetry on page 41, and place over the cake.

Keep-fit class: Cover a round cake with pale yellow sugarpaste. Make marzipan cutouts with small biscuit cutters and attach to the sides with royal icing. Curve them if necessary so they go flat against the cake. Pipe a shell border. Make the figures from marzipan and dress them in marzipan leotards and legwarmers.

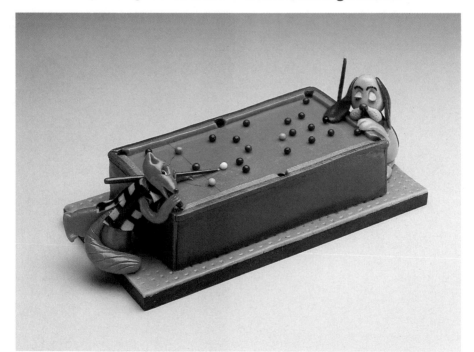

Snooker table cake: Cover a rectangular board with light brown marzipan and mark with a patterned roller. The cake is a 12.5 x 25cm (5 x 10in) rectangle. Cover the sides with brown marzipan and the top with green marzipan. Make narrow strips of brown and green marzipan and put around the top edge, mitring the corners. Cut holes in each corner and in the centre of the long sides with a small round cutter, cutting halfway through the edges. Mark the holes with black marzipan. Make the coloured balls. Make the marzipan cues and leave to harden before positioning. Mark the lines on the table using a pen with edible ink. Position the figures.

Mouse wedding cake: Cover
an oval cake with white sugarpaste. Position a white frill. Make
the three mice and dress them
following the instructions on page
70.

Hallowe'en cake: Coat a round
cake with pale yellow buttercream. Pipe around the top and
base, and divide into sections and
pipe the lines. Position witch,
black cat, jack-o-lantern and
fireworks. Make a small indentation in the centre of the cake and
position the marzipan ghost.